SPORTS

Created by Gallimard Jeunesse
and Pierre-Marie Valat
Illustrated by Pierre-Marie Valat

A FIRST DISCOVERY BOOK

SCHOLASTIC INC.
New York Toronto London Auckland Sydney

There are many different
kinds of sports. Some athletes
are trying to break records:
the longest, the fastest,
the highest, and the heaviest.

Long jump

Sprint

Pole vault

Weight lifting

Cyclists try to
improve speed records
or distance records.

Some skiers race against the clock. Skiing involves speed and flexibility, grace and courage.

Fencers wear masks and
protective clothing.
Their swords are not sharp.

People who compete in the
martial arts also wear
special clothing.

Boxers have to be quick, strong, and light on their feet. The referee makes sure they obey the rules.

Some sports take place on water. These are three-person sculls.

Two people row and the third person calls out commands and sometimes steers.

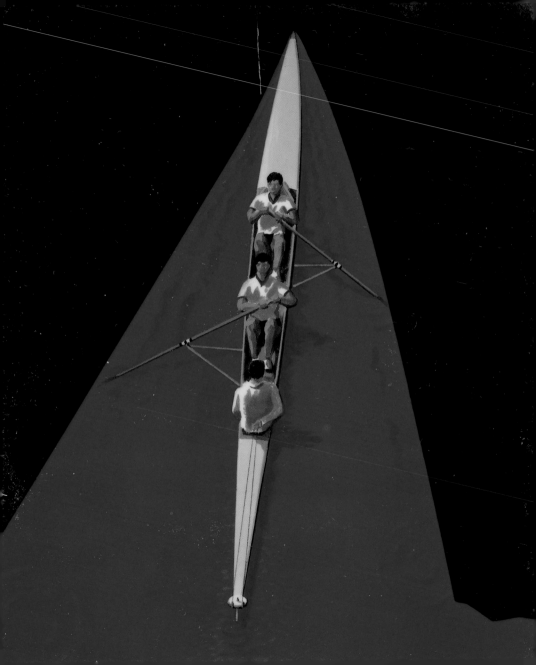

Sailors use the wind to move their boat quickly. Their weight helps to keep the sailboat upright in the water.

When two people play tennis
it is called a singles game.

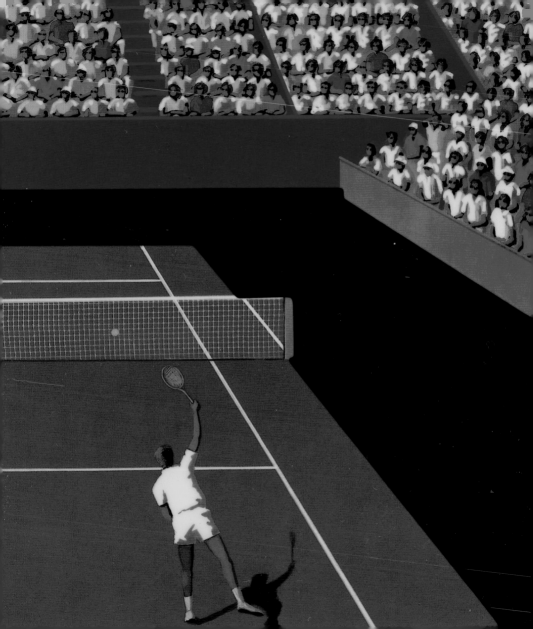

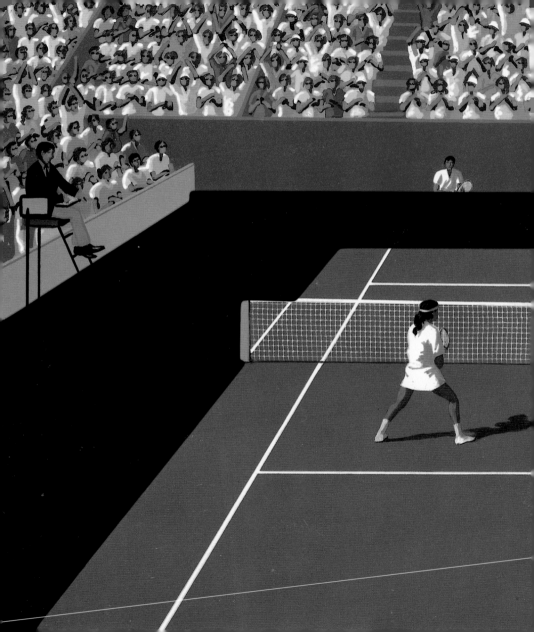

When four people play
it is called doubles.

There are 12 people on a basketball team. Only five teammates play at a time.

Each player has a special talent,
either shooting the ball through the
basket or defending their team's
basket against the other team.

Ice hockey can be very dangerous, so the players wear thick pads and heavy clothing to protect them from harm.

Each team tries to score by shooting the puck past the goalie.

Water polo and team handball are similar sports. Each team tries to put the ball in the other team's net.

Team handball is played on a court.

Water polo is played in a pool.

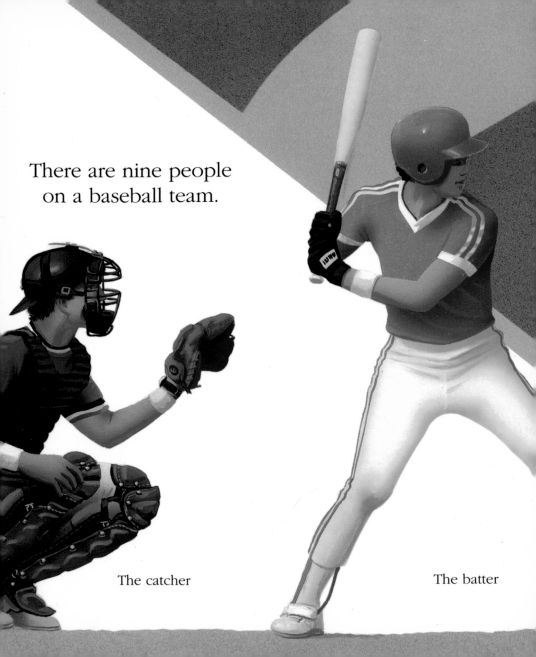

There are nine people
on a baseball team.

The catcher   The batter

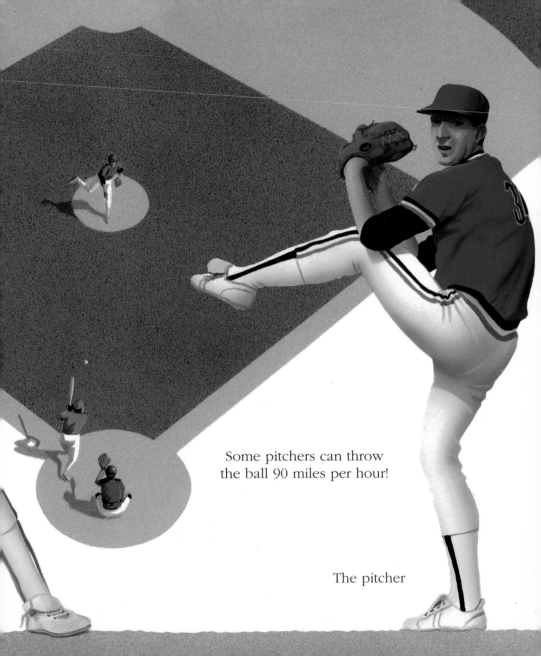

Some pitchers can throw
the ball 90 miles per hour!

The pitcher

There are 11 players on a cricket team.
Each player has a turn at bat. He tries
to hit the ball and knock over the
other team's wicket. The three-legged
wooden piece is the wicket.

The batsman bats.

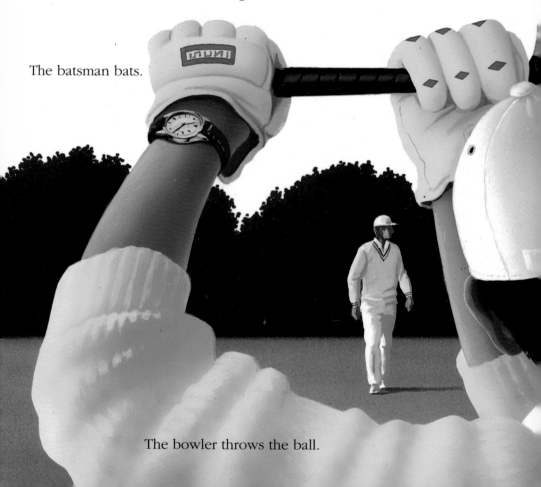

The bowler throws the ball.

In soccer, the goalie tries to block the ball
that is kicked by the other team.

In football, each team has
11 players on the field at a time.

In rugby, like football,
the point of the game is to kick
the ball through the goal or to
carry it over the goal line.

One of the oldest sports is the marathon.

Runners try to finish a race that is more than twenty-six miles long.

Titles in the series of
First Discovery Books:

Airplanes
  and Flying Machines
All About Time
Bears
Bees
Birds
Boats
Butterflies
The Camera
Cars and Trucks
  and Other Vehicles
Castles
Cats
Colors
Construction
Dinosaurs
The Earth and Sky
The Egg
Endangered Animals
Fish

Farm Animals
Flowers
Frogs
Fruit
Horses
Houses
The Human Body
The Ladybug and
  Other Insects
Light
Musical Instruments
Night Creatures
Native Americans
Penguins
Pyramids
The Rain Forest
The River
The Seashore
Sports
Trains
The Tree
Turtles and Snails
Under the Ground

Universe
Vegetables in the
  Garden
Water
Weather
Whales

Titles in the series of
*First Discovery
Art* Books:

Animals
Landscapes
Paintings
Portraits

Titles in the series of
*First Discovery
Atlas* Books:

Atlas of Animals
Atlas of Countries
Atlas of the Earth
Atlas of People
Atlas of Plants

Library of Congress Cataloging-in-Publication Data available.

Originally published in France under the title *Le Sport* by Editions Gallimard Jeunesse.

ISBN 0-590-11617-7

Copyright © 1994 by Editions Gallimard Jeunesse.
This edition English translation by Wendy Barish. Copyright © 1998 by Scholastic Inc.
This edition American text by Wendy Barish. Copyright © 1998 by Scholastic Inc.
This edition Expert Reader: George Sullivan
All rights reserved. First published in the U.S.A. in 1998 by Scholastic Inc. by arrangement with Editions Gallimard Jeunesse, 5 rue Sebastien-Bottin, F-75007, Paris, France.

SCHOLASTIC and A FIRST DISCOVERY BOOK and associated logos are trademarks and/or registered trademarks of Scholastic Inc.

10 9 8 7 6 5 4 3 2 1   8 9/9 0/0 01 02 03

Printed in Italy by Editoriale Libraria
First Scholastic printing, August 1998